DEVON
AND
CORNWALL
RAILWAYS
IN OLD PHOTOGRAPHS

DEVON

AND

CORNWALL RAILWAYS

IN OLD PHOTOGRAPHS

COLLECTED BY

KEVIN ROBERTSON

ALAN SUTTON

Alan Sutton Publishing Limited
Phoenix Mill · Thrupp · Stroud · Gloucestershire

First published 1989
Reprinted 1997
Copyright © 1989 Kevin Robertson

British Library Cataloguing in Publication Data

Devon and Cornwall railways in old photographs.
1. South-west England. Railway services, history
I. Robertson, Kevin
385′.09423

ISBN 0-86299-667-8

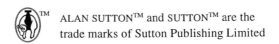
Typesetting and origination by
Alan Sutton Publishing

Printed and bound by
WBC, Bridgend, Mid Glam.

INTRODUCTION

Like many, I have in recent years travelled widely in the areas of Devon and Cornwall and have been fascinated by the signs of its railway past. Within the two counties there is much to comment on, both for the serious railway historian and the more casual visitor, for the area has perhaps witnessed more than its fair share of closures in recent decades.

As an example, it is no longer possible to travel by train to Barnstaple along the scenic route through Dulverton, likewise passage via the Southern line to Plymouth through Okehampton must remain but a memory. Although saddest of all was probably the demise of the narrow gauge Lynton and Barnstaple line in the 1930s. I can only regret that I never had the chance to travel on the route. In this collection of photographs I hope a few memories will be stirred.

I would like to express my thanks to Reg and the gang and also Dennis Tillman for producing the map, also to Judith for her patience at a time when things were not always going well.

KEVIN ROBERTSON
Eastleigh

THE POPULAR IMAGE of the Great Western Railway as the 'holiday line' is captured to advantage here in this publicity photograph of the beach at Dawlish, recorded by the official photographer in 1924. The GWR main line runs in the background and so if one tired of bathing there were always the trains to watch! Records show the view to have been taken in February 1924 and, although the railway attempted a comparison by suggesting the Devon and Cornwall beaches were England's riviera, it can only be assumed that the bathers of the day were a hardy bunch! (GWR)

SPEEDING IN THE WEST. A GWR 'King' class engine at the head of a rake of the latest 'centenary' coaching stock, sometime during the late 1930s.

THE GWR STATION at Exeter St Davids, was hardly situated in the best position to serve the city. Indeed its position was a throwback to the early days of the railway when the new form of transport was not made welcome. Some years later, from 1911–14, the facilities were completely rebuilt, with the new exterior presenting an imposing façade. Of interest in the photograph is the building on the extreme left which for many years served as the carriage sheds for the station. (Lens of Sutton)

SEEN FROM THE LONDON END OF THE PLATFORM at Exeter St Davids is the middle signalbox which dated from 1914. This contained a frame of 95 levers and besides controlling traffic at this end of the station, it was also responsible for the safe movement of road vehicles at the level crossing.

THE YARD GOODS SHED at Exeter St Davids depicted in 1925. Exeter GWR possessed two goods sheds, this being the smaller of the two. Internally it was equipped with two 2-ton cranes. The wagons visible are a 'Mica' van apparently in overall brown livery, together with a small open wagon belonging to the 'Westleigh Stone & Lime Company' of Burlescombe. The latter is fitted with grease axleboxes. (Lens of Sutton)

TAKEN SOME TIME PRIOR TO 1924, this is Exminster station, before the addition of the 'down' loop, looking east towards Exeter. On the left is the station master's house. The generous gap between the running lines is indicative of the former broad gauge lines at the station. (Lens of Sutton)

OPENED IN SEPTEMBER 1912, the station at Dawlish Warren was a popular destination for holiday trippers and replaced a smaller station which had existed nearby from 1912. Most of the facilities were of timber construction and the station was unusually devoid of a protective canopy across the platform. The photograph shows a 'Saint' class 4–6–0 entering the station at the head of a motley collection of stock bound for Exeter, probably not long after the opening. (Lens of Sutton)

SLIGHTLY WEST OF ITS NEIGHBOUR, Dawlish station was also hard by the sea and served the town of the same name, as well as being a popular station in summer months. To the right is the small goods yard which was in use until 1965. In the background are the famous red cliffs through which the railway gently curves via a number of short tunnels. (Lens of Sutton)

MUCH OF THE ORIGINAL RAILWAY alongside the sea wall was single track and had a number of signalboxes controlling the various sections. The one depicted here was at Parsons Tunnel (this and the previous page) just west of Dawlish where the double line of rails converged into one before the route passed through the cliff. Eventually the line was doubled throughout the section to Newton Abbot and as a result the staff instrument shown here became redundant. Reference to early records reveals that in 1896 a 10-lever frame was provided, with the furthest signal being No. 8 – the 'up' distant which was 1,150 yards from the cabin. (Roger Carpenter)

WEST OF DAWLISH and also along the sea shore lies Teignmouth station, seen here probably soon after the abolition of the broad gauge. Notice the train sheds covering part of each platform, which were a feature of many early station designs. These were prone to discolouration by smoke, as well as being a fire risk and so, not surprisingly, they were later removed. (Lens of Sutton)

HEADQUARTERS OF THE LOCOMOTIVE DEPARTMENT of the South Devon railway was at Newton Abbot, which was also the end of the relatively level section of railway from Exeter. From here westwards to Plymouth the route was steeply graded, which was a problem for the steam engineer for many decades. Newton Abbot station was laid out with extensive sidings, part of which can be seen on both sides of the line, while the locomotive depot may be just glimpsed in the right background. (Lens of Sutton)

REBUILDING WORK at Newton Abbot in 1925 (this and the following two pages). The overall roof and cramped facilities were to be swept away and in their place two new island platforms with additional relief lines were provided. The photographs show the work during its early stages. It was to cost the GWR a total of £140,000 before it was completed in 1927. (GWR)

THE IMPOSING EXTERNAL FAÇADE of the rebuilt Newton Abbot station. Access to all the platforms was via this entrance after which a wide and airy staircase and foot-bridge led to the nine platforms and bays. (Lens of Sutton)

TAKEN TO RECORD THE RESULTS OF AN ENEMY AIR RAID at Newton Abbot on Tuesday 20 August 1940. This was the scene on the 'down' main platform looking towards London shortly after the attack. Besides the damage to the structure of the station, a number of locomotives and items of rolling stock were also affected. In terms of human casualties 14 were killed and 61 injured, 15 seriously. (GWR)

SITUATED IN A DIP IN THE GRADIENTS between Newton Abbot and Plymouth, in the valley of the River Dart, Totnes station formed a useful passing place where slow trains might be overtaken in either direction. The photographs are of particular interest, for they clearly show the pumping house erected for the ill-fated atmospheric system, although this was never to be fully operated through the station. The station is seen in its near original form complete with train sheds, both of which were later removed. In the background and out of sight of the camera are the junctions for the Ashburton branch and the short line leading to Totnes quay. (Lens of Sutton)

TAKEN FROM THE ROAD BRIDGE, looking west, a good view is obtained of Brent station, situated part way up the fearsome bank from Totnes. The engine is of interest, being No. 172 *The Abbot* – later No. 2972 which was then running as a 4–4–2, affording a direct comparison with the French engines of the same wheel arrangement acquired by the GWR around that time. (Lens of Sutton)

BRENT was the junction for the Kingsbridge branch also carrying important traffic in the form of livestock. An example of this is depicted here, with what appears to be an 'Armstrong' goods engine adding to the already busy scene at the station. (Lens of Sutton)

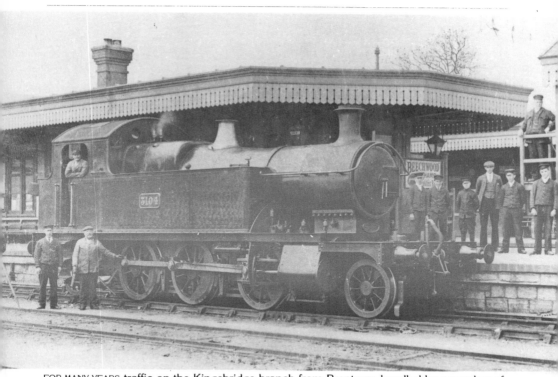

FOR MANY YEARS traffic on the Kingsbridge branch from Brent was handled by a number of small-wheeled 2–6–2 tank engines; two early examples are seen here and overleaf in the shape of Nos. 3104 and 2185. The variations in liveries are of interest as is the cleanliness of both engines. No. 3104 in particular is showing the result of many hours work to produce the mottled effect on the side tanks. (Lens of Sutton)

IN THE BEST RAILWAY TRADITIONS, the station at Ivybridge (this and the following page) was located some little way from the village of the same name and as a result was an early casualty to competition from road traffic. Accordingly it is difficult to appreciate quite why it was deemed necessary to provide as many buildings on the platform as later appeared; the 'up' platform in particular sported a set of neat timber buildings, later a brick waiting shelter was also provided. Just east of the platform the railway was carried across part of the nearby valley, originally by a timber viaduct, later replaced by masonary probably around the turn of the century. (Lens of Sutton)

A DELIGHTFUL VIEW of Plympton station not far from Plymouth and nowadays the scene of much urban development. Adjacent to the station was part of the 4 ft 6 in gauge Plymouth and Dartmoor (Lee moor) tramway which crossed the main line west of the station, as well as at Laira Junction.

DOUBLE-FRAMED 0–6–0 pannier tank No. 1235 on a 'down' local service near to Laira on 14 May 1925. (Lens of Sutton.)

THE FINAL APPROACH to the main GWR station at Plymouth North Road was through the suburb of Mutley, which for some years boasted its own station immediately next to Mutley tunnel. Mutley was a station destined to have a relatively short life, for it opened on 1 August 1871 and was closed 50 years ago on 3 July 1939. (Lens of Sutton)

NORTH ROAD STATION at Plymouth was the most important of the GWR stations in the area. Besides serving the principal Paddington to Penzance trains it also played host to the rival LSWR services *en route* to their own terminus at Plymouth Friary. The photograph shows the North Road station still with its individual train sheds; the facilities were later much altered by rebuilding. (Lens of Sutton)

BESIDES THE STATION AT NORTH ROAD, the GWR possessed a terminus at Plymouth Friary. This was itself a short branch off the line leading to the ocean terminal and docks. Here the exterior of the station is shown with an interesting line up of carriages, possibly indicating the imminent arrival of a main line service. (Lens of Sutton)

TAKING THE GWR ACROSS INTO CORNWALL was Brunel's magnificent Saltash Bridge, the design of which must be well-known to most people. Today it can be seen to advantage from the nearby A38 road bridge. Maintenance was in the hands of a special gang who needed to be agile, as well as not suffer from vertigo! This unusual view is taken from the top of one of the spans, showing the guard and trip rails. The latter are intended to locate against the foot of a workman and so inform him of his position.

THE ROYAL ALBERT BRIDGE – to give its correct title – took the GWR from Devon into Cornwall. Saltash station lies immediately west of the bridge and is the first station in the new county. In this view a steam railmotor complete with an additional trailer car is seen at what is believed to be the station at Millbay. (Lens of Sutton)

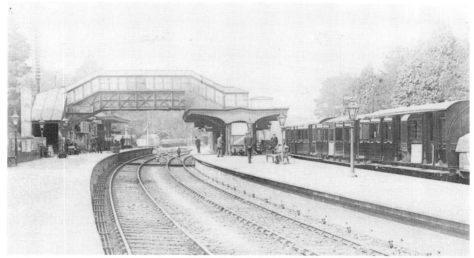

LOOKING WEST TOWARDS PENZANCE this charming view shows the spacious facilities at Bodmin Road. As the station name implies this was hardly convenient for the location of the same name. Trains for the short branch to Bodmin itself used the bay platform on the right. Beyond the station and in the 'V' formed between the main and branch lines, were a number of storage and marshalling sidings. The goods yard proper is just visible on the opposite side of the main route under the foot-bridge. (Lens of Sutton)

FOR MOST OF ITS TIME the GWR led a charmed life, devoid of serious accidents, although the circumstances of 16 April 1895 came within a hair's breadth of being a full disaster for the company. On that date an evening train from Plymouth was running between Doublebois and Bodmin Road when the two engines at its head, Nos. 3521 & 3548 left the rails. The cause was said to be due to the inherently unstable engine design. This paved the way for the rebuilding of the class as tender engines, as well as a slow movement away from using 0–4–4 tank engines for fast passenger work on a number of railway systems.

A VIEW FROM LOSTWITHIEL STATION, looking towards Bodmin Road. Notice in particular the level crossing gates of three differing designs. This is probably indicative of at least one train crashing through the gates in days past.

ALTHOUGH LEASED TO THE SOUTH DEVON COMPANY, the station at Par was originally opened on 4 May 1859 as part of the Cornwall Railway and served from 1879 as a junction for the line to Newquay. The actual point of divergence for the branch is beyond the foot-bridge. Both the Newquay line and to a lesser extent the other nearby line from Fowey generated an amount of goods traffic which was sorted in the goods yard. (Lens of Sutton)

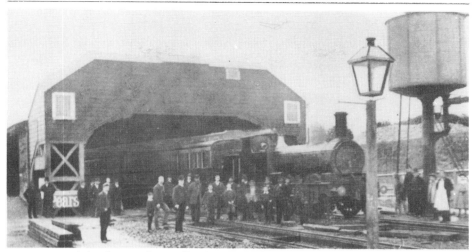

CONVERSION of the former Cornwall railways line from broad to narrow gauge was finally completed in May 1892. This photograph purports to show the arrival of the first narrow gauge train at Truro station.

ONE OF THE MORE IMPORTANT intermediate stations on the Cornwall system was at Truro, which was also the junction for the Falmouth branch services. Three platform faces and a bay were provided and opposite the 'up' loop were extensive sidings. In addition a locomotive shed and turntable were provided and in 1921 became home to an allocation of 19 engines plus a steam railmotor. (Lens of Sutton)

VOLUNTEERS PARADE on the 'up' platform at Redruth, probably recorded c. 1914. The various enamel advertisements are typical of the period, but have slowly disappeared from the railway scene in recent years. In the background are the main station buildings and goods shed. The houses on the left front Bond Street which passes underneath the railway near the end of the platform. (Lens of Sutton)

THE STATION AT CAMBORNE is situated 313½ miles from Paddington. Here it is shown to advantage, looking east towards Redruth. The steam railmotor at the platform is probably bound for Truro. These units more often worked the Truro to Newquay local service and were a rare sight at Camborne station.

AS WITH BODMIN ROAD, the station at Gwinear Road was some three miles from the town from which it took its name, although its importance increased with the opening of the branch to Helston in 1887. This early view is of particular interest as mixed gauge track is evident on the main line, although the branch, on the left, is of narrow gauge track only.

A SLIGHTLY LATER VIEW of Gwinear Road station, photographed looking towards Penzance in 1920. Notice the timber station buildings and now standard gauge track, also the barren background, typical of certain parts of west Cornwall. (Lens of Sutton)

COMPLETE WITH ITS ORNATE PALM TREES, the station at St Erth was just 5½ miles from Penzance and the commencement of yet another of the numerous branch lines in the county, this time to St Ives. In this view the cameraman has his back to the branch line and is looking west, the main station buildings are on the right. (Lens of Sutton)

PENZANCE STATION, 326½ miles from Paddington, equal to perhaps 9½ hours by train in steam days. Doubling of the final section of line as far as Penzance station was eventually completed as late as 1921. The restricted area around the station meant goods and locomotive facilities were some little way east at Ponsandane and Long Rock. (Lens of Sutton)

AS AN ADDITIONAL SERVICE, the GWR operated a 'road motor' between Penzance and Lands End during a variety of dates between 1904 and 1928. In this view taken shortly after the service started, two Milnes-Daimler 20 hp vehicles are seen, both with Milnes bodies. They were delivered for service in the spring of 1904. (Lens of Sutton)

A DELIGHTFUL PUBLICITY PHOTOGRAPH of the sands at Exmouth which, despite being taken by the GWR official photographer, depicted a location only served by the rival Southern Railway company! The fashions of the day are worthy of study, as is the gentleman partly hidden in the large hole in the sand!

ANOTHER OF THE BRANCH LINES off the South Western main line to Exeter diverged at Sidmouth Junction, with the main station shown here. From the platform on the left trains would leave for Sidmouth as well as Budleigh and Exmouth, the latter location was also served direct from Exeter by trains running via Topsham. (Lens of Sutton)

Axminster. LSWR.

ON THE RIVAL SOUTH WESTERN LINE into Devon and Cornwall, is Axminster station (this and the following page). Besides serving the town of the same name it was also the junction for the little branch to Lyme Regis. Architecturally the station was similar to a number on the west of England main line and, as well as its passenger traffic it dealt with quantities of carpet from the factory in the town. (Lens of Sutton)

SEATON JUNCTION STATION was the next station on from Axminster and is seen here in its original form with just an 'up' and 'down' main line. In the period 1927/8 the amenities were completely rebuilt with additional through lines, while a separate platform was also provided for the Seaton branch services. (Lens of Sutton)

A CHARMING PERIOD VIEW of Whimple station looking towards Salisbury, probably during the Edwardian era. The photograph was taken to illustrate the new foot-bridge, which was erected before concrete became a standard component for such structures on the Southern.

WEST OF WHIMPLE was the station at Broadclyst. The word 'clyst' is used as part of the name for various villages around the Exeter area. The photographs show the station from both directions, with the goods yard at the London end. A wagon turntable was provided here probably from the time the station opened, although this was removed by 1920. (Lens of Sutton)

SERVING THE INTERESTS OF THE SOUTH WESTERN at Exeter was the station at Queen Street, which in recent years has been renamed Exeter Central (this and the following four pictures). Here the main line engine, which had brought the 'West of England' express from Waterloo, would be detached and the train would continue west behind a smaller engine. Accordingly facilities were provided for carriage and wagon storage, as well as locomotive requirements at nearby Exmouth Junction. The line continued west down a fearsome gradient to join the GWR at St Davids station before running north to diverge at Cowley Bridge for Crediton and former LSWR lines in Devon and Cornwall. (Lens of Sutton)

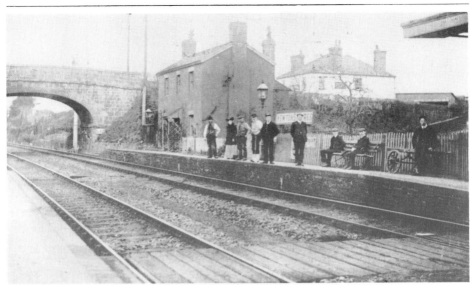

ORIGINALLY PART OF A BROAD GAUGE LINE which passed into the hands of the LSWR, the station at Newton St Cyres opened in 1851. It is seen here possibly around the turn of the century with what is probably the station master's house visible at the end of the platform. (Lens of Sutton)

ANOTHER STATION showing its origins lie more with the GWR was that at Crediton (this and the following photograph), which later had the steam engine No. 34048 named after it. Notice the diamond shape of the chimneys on the buildings, which would appear to be unusual for the railway architecture of the area. (Lens of Sutton)

SOUTHERN RAILWAY enquiry and publicity stand at the agricultural show at Crediton in June 1926. (Lens of Sutton)

WEST OF CREDITON the Plymouth line diverges from the north Devon lines at Coleford Junction; the first station on the Plymouth section being that at Bow. Here the main buildings were constructed from local stone and are in keeping with similar amenities provided at LSWR wayside stations on various parts of the system. (Lens of Sutton)

SIMILAR TO BOW was the next station at North Tawton, both fringing the northern slopes of what is now the Dartmoor National Park. Facilities here were in existence from 1865 onwards. The crowd on the platform was probably an outing recorded for posterity by the camera. (Lens of Sutton)

MOST IMPORTANT OF ALL THE STATIONS on the LSWR Plymouth route was Okehampton, near to where the railway also established a large granite quarry to service its needs for ballast. The quarry is still serving the same need today although the line to Plymouth is truncated at this point. In this view a train of obvious military significance has arrived at Okehampton station and is seen split into three parts. It is likely this was some time during the First World War. (Lens of Sutton)

THE NEAREST STATION to the peak of Yes Tor was at Bridestowe, on what is now the closed section of the former LSWR Plymouth main line. In the photograph a Drummond 4–4–0 is arriving at the station, the engine temporarily fitted with cross tubes to the firebox. (Lens of Sutton)

PERMANENT WAY STAFF and equipment at work near Brentor (LSWR) in July 1927. (Lens of Sutton)

TAVISTOCK once boasted two stations; the GWR station on the floor of the valley, part way along the Launceston branch from Plymouth while the LSWR route traversed the countryside high above the town and as a result a high stone viaduct was required. There was no physical connection between the two lines in the town. (Lens of Sutton)

LOCATED NEAR THE UPPER REACHES of the Tamar river, the station at Bere Alston also served as the junction for the Callington branch. In this view looking north towards Okehampton the platform appears well patronized, while the various items of infrastructure depict a typical LSWR style. (Lens of Sutton)

TYPICAL OF THE LSWR LINES in Devon and Cornwall were sharp curves and steep gradients, both seen here as No. 311 works hard, near what is believed to be Bere Ferrers, with an express passenger service. (Lens of Sutton)

THE DELIGHTFULLY NAMED TAMERTON FOLIAT station on the banks of the Tamar, not far from the meeting of the LSWR and GWR systems at Plymouth. (Lens of Sutton)

— Side Elevation —

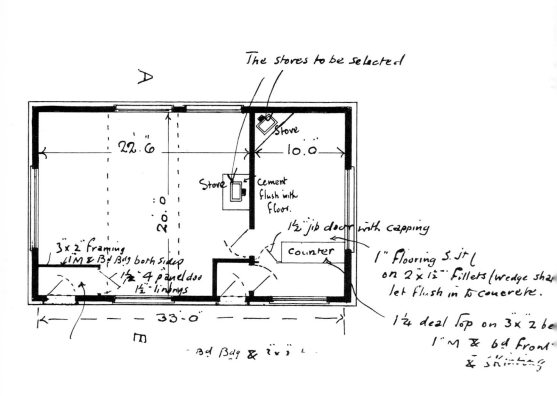

A

The stores to be selected

22'.6   Store

10.0

Store   Cement
         flush with
         floor.

20'.0

½" jib door with capping

3 x 2" framing   Counter
∠ IM & Bd B'g both sides
½" 4 panel door   1" Flooring S. J'T
½" linings   on 2 x 1½" fillets (wedge shape
                        let flush in to concrete.

33'-0"   1¼ deal top on 3 x 2 be

B   1" M & bd Front
                        & skirting
- Bd B'g & ı x ı ∟ -

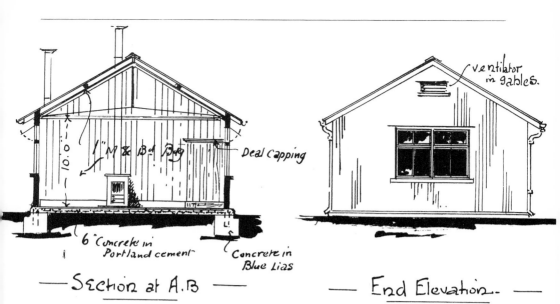

Section at A.B —   — **End Elevation.** —

ventilator in gables.

Deal capping

1" M & Bd Btg

10.0

6" Concrete in Portland cement

Concrete in Blue Lias

NOTE. Drainage to be arranged on the ground. 4" pipes

&SWR. DEVONPORT STATION.

Goods Staff. Offices.

Feet 10   5   0   10   20   30 feet

Scale of Feet.

THERE WERE ORIGINALLY TWO STATIONS at St Budeaux (Plymouth), although it was not until BR days that a suffix was added to differentiate between the two. (Lens of Sutton)

AFTER RUNNING THROUGH the rivals' station at North Road, LSWR trains would make their way along the final distance to their own terminus at Plymouth Friary. The station seen here as a hive of activity, with at least four steam engines visible. (Lens of Sutton)

AN ADAM'S DESIGN ENGINE at Halwill Junction and Beauworthy station, the junction for the lines to Bude and Padstow. The design of the signal is of interest, having the typical LSWR diamond lattice-work, with what appears to be a solid core within. (Lens of Sutton)

HALWILL JCT. LSWR 3/7/05.

THREE PHOTOGRAPHS (this and the page opposite) of the accident at Halwill Junction on 3 July 1905. There is scant reference in official sources to this accident. Seeing the various vehicles involved from unusual angles, it is possible to pick up some interesting detail including the wheels with split spokes. (Lens of Sutton)

HALWILL J. L.S.W.R. 3/7/05.

LWILL J. L.S.W.R. 3/7/05

A SLIGHTLY LATER VIEW at Halwill, this time with a 'T9' 4–4–0 at the platform resplendent in clean green livery. (Lens of Sutton)

A MEETING OF THE RIVALS at Launceston, which was the terminus of the GWR line from Plymouth, while the LSWR route continued west towards Padstow. The station was unusual in that it had a joint signalbox. During the 1940s a physical connection was provided for the first time to join the two routes. (Lens of Sutton)

TWO PHOTOGRAPHS OF CHILSWORTHY STATION on the Plymouth, Devonport and South Western branch from Bere Alston to Callington. This was an independent company, absorbed by the LSWR in 1922, and subsequently the SR in the following year, which owned two unusual design 0–6–2 tank locomotives. One is seen at Chilsworthy station with another in the next view. (Lens of Sutton)

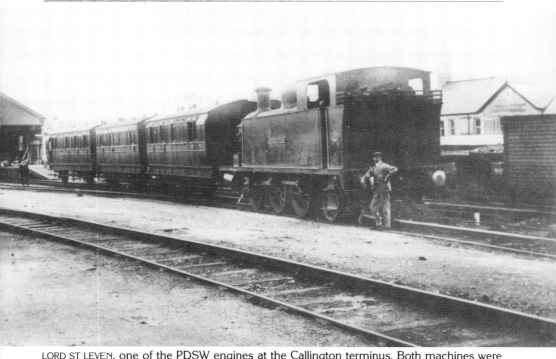

LORD ST LEVEN, one of the PDSW engines at the Callington terminus. Both machines were taken over from the Southern by BR in 1948 and survived in use for some years, although not necessarily on the line for which they had been built. (Lens of Sutton)

THE TERMINUS AT CALLINGTON with its typical, if rather optimistic, advertising board. (Lens of Sutton)

NORTH NOW FROM YEOFORD JUNCTION towards Barnstaple and Ilfracombe, with the first station on this line, seen here, at Copplestone. Notice the platform devoid of any protective canopy, while the provision of a water tower was unusual at a country stopping place. (Lens of Sutton)

ANOTHER STATION on the line to Barnstaple was that of Lapford. Here the main buildings appear to have an unusual form of protection on the platform side. (Lens of Sutton)

BARNSTAPLE TOWN STATION depicted in May 1925. Both the GWR and LSWR had stations in the town, this being the LSWR stopping place.

FOUR VIEWS OF BARNSTAPLE TOWN STATION (this and the following three photographs) which was also the terminus of the narrow gauge branch from Lynton. (Lens of Sutton)

BARNSTAPLE JCT. LSWR

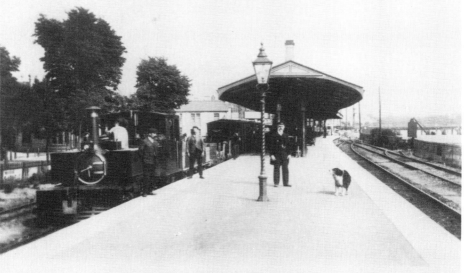

S 2942 BARNSTAPLE TOWN STATION.

A DELIGHTFUL VIEW of SR No. 762, *Lyn*, which was built by the American firm of Balwins. The engine is seen in the process of running around at Barnstaple.

A DOUBLE-HEADED MIXED TRAIN waiting to leave Barnstaple for Lynton, sometime after 1923.
(Lens of Sutton)

THE L & B YARD AT PILTON, where locomotives and rolling stock were stabled and serviced. The area here is now an industrial estate. (Lens of Sutton)

LEW in need of a helping hand after a minor derailment. It must be a matter of considerable regret that this line failed to survive, being closed by the SR during the economies of the 1930s. It would surely have been a popular tourist attraction 50 years on. (Lens of Sutton)

BRAUNTON STATION also had an engine named after it, however, this was not until some years after both these photographs were taken. The station was situated north of Wrafton on the final section to Ilfracombe and portrays beautifully the impression of a country stopping place. (Lens of Sutton)

BEYOND BARNSTAPLE the standard gauge line forks to either Torrington or Ilfracombe, with one of the stations on the latter route, Wrafton, shown here. The railway here was fairly close to the North Devon coast and so was a popular destination for holiday makers in the summer season. The SR was quick to recognize this and so placed some camping coaches at the station. (Lens of Sutton)

THE FINAL STATION before Ilfracombe was at Mortehoe, which also served the resort of Woolacombe. Notice the similarity in station architecture compared with the views of several other North Devon stations. The position of the signalbox in the centre of the platform probably allowed for a porter/signalman's post at the station. (Lens of Sutton)

FACING THE ATLANTIC COAST, the terminus at Ilfracombe was the final destination for many who had started their journey at Waterloo and as such was equipped to deal with holiday trains. Notice the extensive siding accommodation. In winter, however, the site could become very bleak, as depicted below, with an extensive covering of snow. (Lens of Sutton)

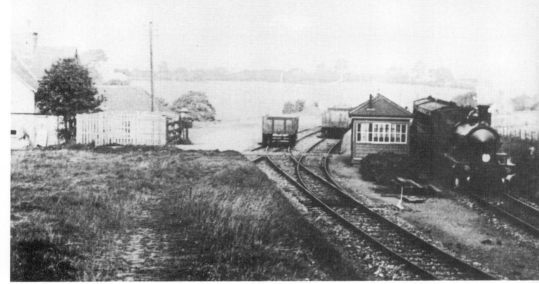

COMBPYNE, LSWR.

MOVING EAST AGAIN it is now appropriate to take a brief look at some of the LSWR branch lines situated off the main line before reaching Exeter. The first of these is the Lyme Regis line. This started from Axminster station and had just the one intermediate stopping place at Combpyne – seen here. Because of its sharp curves, the route was for many years the province of the Adam's radial tank engines of 4–4–2 wheel arrangement. One of these is seen here leaving the diminutive stopping place with a train for Lyme Regis. (Lens of Sutton)

OPENING DAY of the Axminster–Lyme Regis branch on 24 August 1903, with two LSWR 'Terriers' Nos. 734 and 735 on one of the first trains at the terminus. (Lens of Sutton)

COLYTON STATION on the branch from Seaton Junction to Seaton. Here the station is shown in relationship to the town; engineering work is in progress at the site. The station here was opened as Colyton Town in 1868, although the suffix was dropped from around 1890 onwards. (Lens of Sutton)

THE TERMINUS OF THE BRANCH was at Seaton, just a short distance from the sea. As with so many of the branch lines leading down to the coast, traffic was seasonal, the station staff are seen here apparently awaiting the next influx of trippers. (Lens of Sutton)

A DELIGHTFUL VIEW of the level crossing at Cadhay near Ottery St Mary. The gates were hand operated, with a small cottage provided for the crossing keeper, who would also have to lower the signals by means of the lever frame when the line was clear for the passage of a train. (Lens of Sutton)

THE BRANCH TRAIN entering Ottery St Mary station at the head of which appears to be an '02' tank engine. The various costumes worn by the passengers are worthy of a second look. (Lens of Sutton)

AT TIPTON ST JOHNS the line split, one section going on to Sidmouth, the other continuing around the coast to Budleigh Salterton and eventually Exmouth. This view looks towards the junction of the two lines, with the ground level signalbox controlling the actual divergence, just visible in the distance. (Lens of Sutton)

THERE WERE NO INTERMEDIATE STATIONS between Tipton and Sidmouth, instead the line terminated at the latter, in what was for many years basically a rural area. Notice the alternate pink and brown livery for the canopy valance and also the engine shed. A loco was stabled here most nights in preparation for the first train service in the morning (this and the following photograph). (Lens of Sutton)

The Railway Station, Sidmouth.

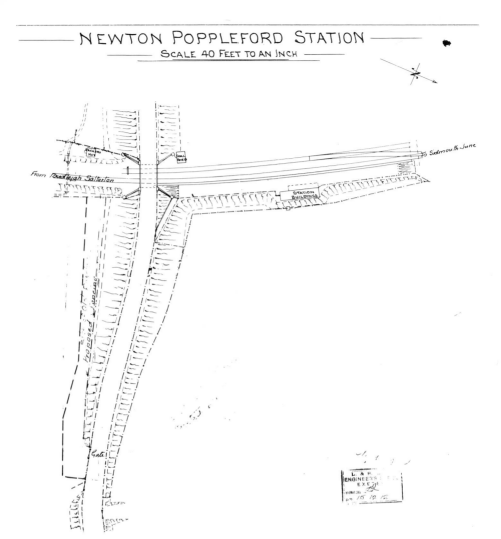

PROPOSED FENCING on the approach to the delightfully named Newton Poppleford station on the line from Tipton to Budleigh, 1912.

THE ORIGINAL BRIDGE No. 24 over the railway near Budleigh Salterton, 12 March 1923.

TRAVELLING NORTH NOW FROM EXMOUTH the railway passes through Lympstone before coming to the station at Woodbury Road. Notice the tile-hung building on the right. The presence of what would appear to be main line coaching stock, indicates that this may well be a through train to or from Waterloo. (Lens of Sutton)

EXMOUTH was served by lines from both Budleigh and Exeter, the latter running via Topsham. The station buildings reflected the importance the SR placed on the station. It was rebuilt in the form shown soon after 1923. Unfortunately, changing traffic needs have meant the station is today altered almost beyond recognition, being served only by the line through Topsham. The structure shown here has been demolished to make way for a bus stop and car park. (Lens of Sutton)

THE STATION AT TOPSHAM was also the end of the double line section from Exmouth Junction (Exeter). Leading down from the railway here a short branch served the harbour, while the station was ideally situated to serve the town close by.

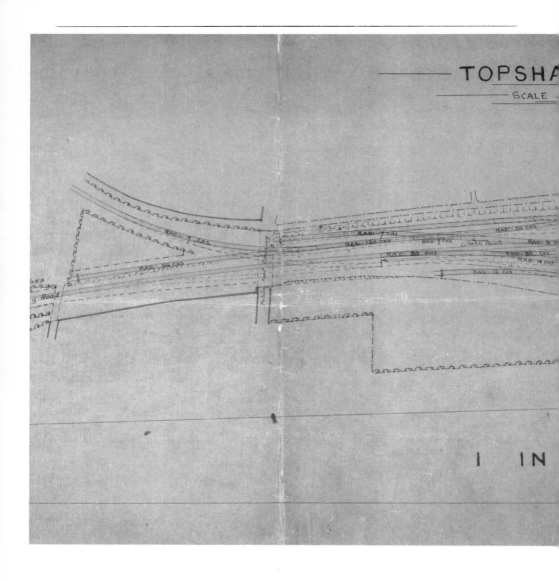

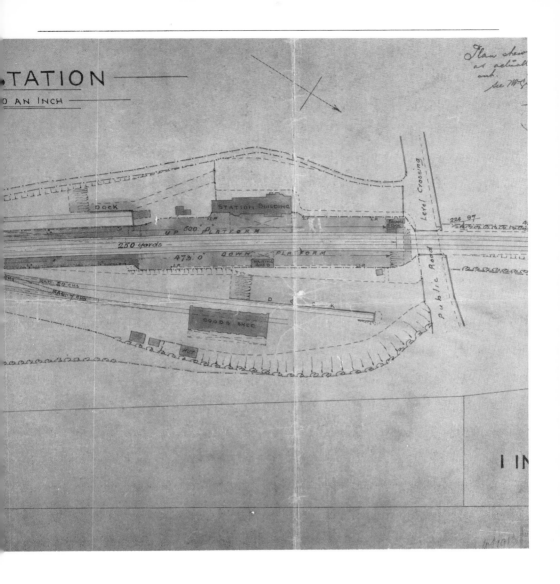

ALTHOUGH NOT STRICTLY IN DEVON, I could not resist the inclusion of this superb view of Milverton station on the long GWR branch from Taunton to Barnstaple. The view does much to epitomize the rural branch line scene, with the pick-up goods train waiting in the platform and the crew deep in conversation with the signalman. (Lens of Sutton)

ACROSS THE BORDER into Devon proper was Morebath station, not to be confused with the halt of similar name a few miles further west. The GWR Taunton to Barnstaple branch was basically a single line railway with passing loops at the various stations. (Lens of Sutton)

MOST IMPORTANT of all the intermediate stations between Taunton and Barnstaple was Dulverton, seen here to advantage in these two photographs. Despite serving what was primarily a rural area there was a reasonable amount of traffic. Much of this was in the form of agricultural traffic, examples of which can be seen in the yard. (Lens of Sutton)

TIMBER being dealt with at Dulverton station. (Lens of Sutton)

A PICTURESQUE VIEW of Bampton Station on the Exe Valley line. The train is probably from Exeter and is heading towards Morebath Junction and Dulverton. Notice particularly the ivy-clad station buildings and also the enclosed canopy between the two wings of the main building. An extensive goods yard was also located here.

WEST OF DULVERTON the railway eventually came to South Molton station, not to be confused with South Molton Road station on the LSWR line to Barnstaple. An average of seven passenger trains ran in each direction on weekdays, with additional trains on Fridays. (Lens of Sutton)

OPENED ORIGINALLY in 1885 as Cadeleigh & Bickleigh, the name was simplified to just Cadeleigh from May 1906 onwards. The view looks north towards Tiverton and was probably taken some time soon after 1929. Notice the lime-washed lower portions of the cattle wagon and also the curved diamond crossing. Protecting the exit from the yard, a catch point and its point disc can also be seen. (Lens of Sutton)

FIRST OF THE INTERMEDIATE STATIONS on the Hemyock branch from Tiverton Junction was at Uffculme, which dealt with passenger traffic for some 87 years, from the time of opening in 1876. The station was ideally situated for the village of the same name and dealt with cattle traffic as well as quantities of milk. (Lens of Sutton)

SOUTH OF EXETER now and on to the predominantly single track branch line from City Basin Junction to Newton Abbot. Besides its branch line status, this was a useful diversionary route for main line trains in the event of disruption to services along the exposed coastal route through Dawlish. Ide station is shown here, which was the first of the stopping places south of Exeter. (Lens of Sutton)

CONTINUING ON TOWARDS NEWTON ABBOT is the station at Christow, with its crossing loop and small goods yard clearly visible. The line was opened in 1903 and closed to passengers in 1958 after a life of just 55 years. (Lens of Sutton)

ONE OF THE DIFFICULTIES in using the Exeter railway, as it was called, for diversions was its ruling gradient of 1 in 56 and as a result, after nationalization, it was the former SR route from Plymouth through Okehampton that found favour. Consequently the branch traffic remained minimal and there was little outward change to the traffic dealt with at stations like Chudleigh over the years.

TWO VIEWS (this and the following page) of the little stopping place at Trusham, complete with its rather unusually designed signalbox. The well-kept station gardens show up particularly well on the platform, while the bridge is clearly wide enough for a second line of rails should this have ever proved necessary. (Lens of Sutton)

TRUSHAM. GWR

BOVEY TRACEY G.W.R.

ANOTHER LINE to terminate at Newton Abbot was the branch from Moretonhampstead, which opened in 1866 (this and the next three photographs). There were four intermediate stations, with Heathfield forming a junction with the Exeter railway from 1903 onwards. Opened originally as a broad gauge line, the remnants of this can be seen from the photograph showing the baulk road at Bovey Tracey, although this was eventually replaced by cross sleepers at a later date. For some years the GWR also operated a bus service from Bovey Tracey during the summer season to a variety of tourist destinations, including the Becky Falls and Haytor Rocks. (Lens of Sutton)

ABOVE BOVEY came Lustleigh station, seen here with a 'Metro' tank at the head of a train of five 4-wheeled coaches. (Lens of Sutton)

LOCATED on what is now the privately operated Torbay Steam Railway, the station at Churston was once the junction for trains to Brixham, a service which has not now operated for nearly 30 years. Trains on the branch would start from the bay platform on the left. A small waiting shelter was provided for the convenience of passengers on the branch line. Notice also the 'Railway Hotel' in the background. (Lens of Sutton)

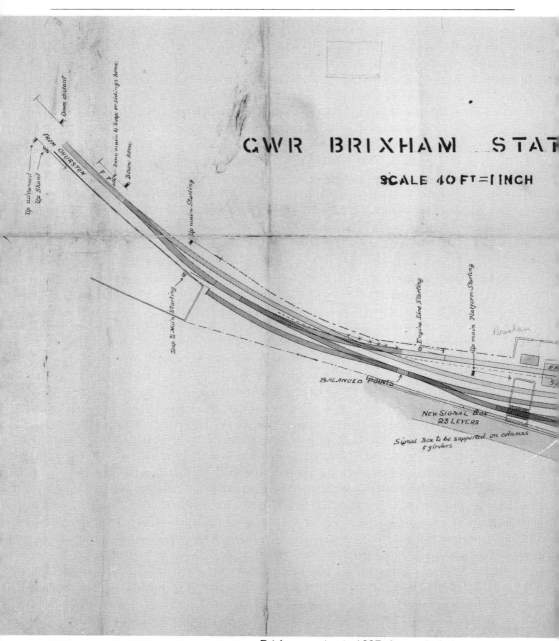

SCALE 40 FT = 1 INCH

Down distant

from CHURSTON

Up advanced
Up Shunt

F ph
Down main to loop or sidings home
Down home

Up main Starting

loop to Main Starting

Engine Line Starting

Up main Platform Starting

Brixham

BALANCED POINTS

NEW SIGNAL BOX
23 LEVERS

Signal Box to be supported on columns & girders

PROPOSED ALTERATIONS AND EXTENSIONS to Brixham station in 1897; they included an 'up and over' signalbox which was never built.

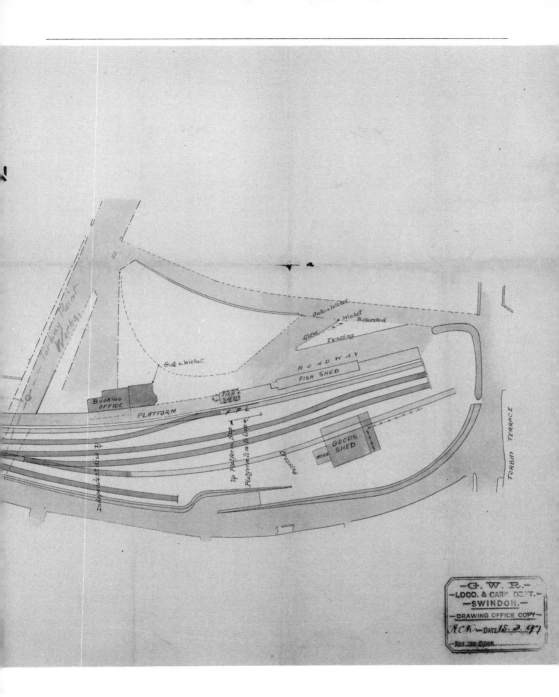

DARTMOUTH — THE STATION WITH NO TRAINS

ACROSS THE RIVER FROM KINGSWEAR lay the town of Dartmouth, where the GWR provided a fine station but no rail access! Instead passengers were conveyed by ferry across to Kingswear. The *Mew* a small tug-type vessel was utilized by the railway for some years. (Lens of Sutton)

NORTH FROM TOTNES ON THE MUCH LOVED Dart Valley branch was the Ashburton terminus. Notice the wooden train shed — a feature of many branch line termini. Ashburton was unusual in that it never boasted a signalbox, having instead a solitary starting signal operated from a small ground frame, which controlled trains leaving the station. (Lens of Sutton)

PART OF THE ASHBURTON BRANCH survives today as the Dart Valley railway. The photograph shows Buckfastleigh station as it was for many years with an unidentified 14xx tank engine on the return working from Ashburton. Regretfully much of the character of the site has now changed following the building of the A38 trunk road. (Lens of Sutton)

AVONWICK STATION, looking 'up' the branch towards Brent in 1921. At the end of the platform can be seen, the ground frame which controlled the entry into the small goods yard. The canopy extends the full width of the platform and was of a style seen at several small branch line stations. (Lens of Sutton)

A KINGSBRIDGE BRANCH TRAIN travelling through the woods near to Avonwick and with a '517' class engine at its head. (Lens of Sutton)

ANOTHER VIEW OF AVONWICK STATION this time with a '517' class 0–4–2 tank at the head of the branch service. (Lens of Sutton)

Loddiswell. GWR

TWO VIEWS OF LODDISWELL STATION on the Kingsbridge branch, looking towards Kingsbridge. In the distance can be seen the station master's house. The GWR colour scheme of 'light and dark' stone also shows up well on the canopy valancing. (Lens of Sutton)

Loddiswell. 14/6/21.

MARSH MILLS. G.W.R.

A 44XX SERIES 'PRAIRIE' TANK at Marsh Mills on the Launceston branch from Plymouth, seen at the head of some steel-hopper ballast wagons. (Lens of Sutton)

THE TERMINUS OF THE BRANCH AT KINGSBRIDGE (this and the following three photographs) with a good general view of the station and its environs. Facilities included the usual goods and passenger landings, as well as a small carriage shed and locomotive shed. For many years rabbits were a major part of the traffic handled and amounted to up to 25 tons of traffic weekly. (Lens of Sutton)

ingsbridge.

THE TERMINUS AT YEALMPTON (this and the opposite page) was at the end of a short branch from Plymouth and suffered a chequered history before finally closing in 1960. Originally opened in January 1898 the passenger service was withdrawn as early as 1930, only to be restored again between 1941 and 1947. For some years a GWR sponsored road motor service also operated in the area, but this too failed to assist in generating additional traffic. (Lens of Sutton)

YEALMPTON STATION

ON THE WAY TO BIGBURY-ON-SEA, YEALMPTON STATION. C.CI.

THE DELIGHTFULLY PICTURESQUE STATION at Yelverton, which was also the junction for the little branch to Princetown, high on Dartmoor (this and the following three photographs). At the north end of the platform the branch line joined the 'main line' after which the route plunged into a tunnel. Yelverton was one of the places where gravity shunting was employed, which involved the Princetown train pushing its coaches up the branch before running clear into a siding after which the empty vehicles would descend into the platform under the control of the guard. This manoeuvre is depicted in one of the accompanying photographs. (Lens of Sutton)

YELVERTON. G.W.

THE RUGGED BEAUTY OF THE MOORS near Yelverton station, with a GWR bus just visible climbing the road in the distance.

A DELIGHTFUL PICTURE of the branch train service near Yelverton station in 1905.

DOUSLAND STATION on the branch from Yelverton to Princetown. Here the advertisement for 'Teas, Hot Water and Mineral Water' would appear to be more prominent than the railway itself! (Lens of Sutton)

THE BLEAK TERMINUS of the branch at Princetown (this and the following two photographs). Often the only means of travel to the town during winter months was by train. Prisoners for internment at Dartmoor would also arrive here, the station seeing a regular 'clientele' for the establishment which had first been built to hold Frenchmen captured during the Napoleonic wars. (Lens of Sutton)

NORTH OF YELVERTON, towards Launceston, the railway passes through the station at Horrabridge. The photograph is of a Plymouth bound train, with most of the yard invisible behind the engine and carriages. (Lens of Sutton)

ON THE WESTERN FRINGES of Devon was Coryton station, not to be confused with Colyton on the LSWR Seaton branch (this and the following page), which boasted just a single platform, although there was a small goods yard at the Launceston end of the station. Controlling the points into the siding was a covered ground frame, which can be seen to the front of the trains. (Lens of Sutton)

LIFTON STATION, located next to what is now the busy A30 main road, owed much of its business to a creamery built alongside the railway, to which a private siding provided access. The two photographs depict the scene before and after the extension of facilities and make for an interesting comparison. The house in the foreground was built for the station master. (Lens of Sutton)

otor Cars. Saltash to Callington.

GWR ROAD MOTORS used on the Saltash to Callington service. (Lens of Sutton)

Looe 31/5/22.

THE LITTLE STATION AT LOOE, situated on the extreme end of what was originally part of a Cornish mineral railway. Trains destined to serve the branch would leave the main line at Liskeard before dropping down and reversing under a high viaduct to gain access to it. (Lens of Sutton)

FOWEY STATION. Geological constraints dictated the railway had to be laid on a sharp curve and as a result check rails are provided. Notice the leather background to the token set-down point and its associated cow horn. The latter item was still available ex-stock from BR signal stores as late at 1988! (Lens of Sutton)

WITH ITS CHARACTERISTIC STEEP THOROUGHFARES the village of Brodinnick, which lies across the river from Fowey, is still recognizable today. The photograph was one purportedly taken by the railway's publicity department to emphasize the charm of the area.

BUGLE STATION on the line from Par through to Newquay, was the junction of two of the Cornish mineral lines; to Carbis and Gunheath. In this 1931 photograph the view is surprisingly devoid of people and movement. Notice the china clay heaps in the background.

A FAVOURITE DESTINATION for many trippers was that of Newquay. The long platforms of the station indicate that it often enjoyed busy periods. Today trains still serve the station, although the service is but a shadow of its former self, with diesel units and HST sets the mainstay of the service. (Lens of Sutton)

A CHARMING VIEW OF THE STATION at Shepherds on the long branch from Newquay towards Chasewater, which was also the junction for further mineral lines to Treamble and Gravel Hill. There is much of interest in the picture, including the GWR station seat, staff uniforms and travelling safe – the rectangular box on the platform at the far end of the main building. (Lens of Sutton)

A STEAM ENGINE and solitary auto coach form the branch service at St Agnes station not far from the northern coast of Cornwall. This was another popular station at holiday times. (Lens of Sutton)

FROM TRURO on the main line an important branch led off to the port of Falmouth, the harbour of which is seen in the background. Notice the baulk road and also the 'siphon' van, the latter intended for the carriage of milk in churns, with slats provided to induce air flow and so hopefully keep the contents cooled. (Lens of Sutton)

THE FINAL BRANCH north of the main line to Plymouth was that leading to St Ives. One of its two intermediate stations, Lelant, is shown here. The ornamental station lamp would now be a collectors item, although at the time it is interesting to note that the picture reveals no signs of vandalism anywhere on the site. (Lens of Sutton)

THE FINAL PORT OF CALL in this brief look at the railways of the area is at Helston, the end of the branch from Gwinear Road. Traffic at this obscure outpost of the GWR was largely based on seasonal broccoli, which necessitated special trains at picking time. The branch opened in May 1887, with goods traffic finally withdrawn in 1962. (Lens of Sutton)

OPENING OF LINES IN DATE ORDER

4. 7.1834	Bodmin to Wadebridge
1. 5.1844	Bristol to Exeter
30.12.1846	Exeter to Newton Abbot
12. 6.1848	Tiverton Road (Junction) to Tiverton
18.12.1848	Newton Abbot to Torquay
12. 5.1851	Exeter to Crediton
25. 8.1852	Penzance to Truro
1. 8.1854	Crediton to Fremington
2.11.1855	Fremington to Bideford
24. 9.1858	Lee Moor Tramway
4. 5.1859	Cornwall Railway
4. 5.1859	Royal Albert Bridge, Saltash
22. 6.1859	Plymouth to Tavistock
1. 8.1859	Torre to Paignton
19. 7.1870	Yeovil to Exeter
27.12.1860	Liskeard and Looe
14. 3.1861	Dartmouth and Torbay Railway
1. 5.1861	Exeter to Exmouth
1. 2.1862	Exeter Queen Street to Exeter St Davids
24. 8.1863	Falmouth Branch
1. 7.1865	Tavistock to Launceston
4. 7.1866	Moretonhampstead and South Devon
28. 2.1868	Brixham Branch
16. 3.1868	Seaton and Bere Railway
1. 6.1869	Lostwithiel to Fowey
1. 7.1869	Newquay and Cornwall Junction
3.10.1871	North Tawton to Okehampton
1. 5.1872	Totnes to Ashburton
7. 5.1872	Bere Alston to Callington
18. 7.1872	Bideford to Torrington
1.11.1873	Wiveliscombe to Barnstaple
1. 6.1874	Cornwall Minerals Railway

6. 7.1874	Sidmouth Branch
20. 7.1874	Barnstaple to Ilfracombe
12.10.1874	Okehampton to Lydford
1. 6.1876	Tiverton Junction to Hemyock
1. 6.1877	St Erth to St Ives
20. 1.1879	Meldon Junction to Holsworthy
9.10.1882	Teign Valley Railway
11. 8.1883	Princetown Branch
1. 8.1884	Tiverton to Morebath Junction
1. 5.1885	Tiverton to Stoke Canon
21. 7.1886	Halwill to Launceston
9. 5.1887	Helston Branch
1. 6.1890	PDSW via Tavistock and Bere Alston
28. 7.1892	Launceston to Tresmeer
5. 9.1892	Turnchapel Branch
14. 8.1893	Tresmeer to Camelford
18.10.1893	Camelford to Delabole
19.12.1893	Kingsbridge Branch
1. 6.1895	Delabole to Wadebridge
1.11.1895	Wadebridge to Bodmin
15. 5.1897	Budleigh Salterton Railway
19. 1.1898	Yealmpton Branch
16. 5.1898	Lynton and Barnstaple Railway
11. 8.1898	Holsworthy to Bude
27. 3.1899	Wadebridge to Padstow
25. 2.1901	Looe line to Liskeard
1. 6.1903	Exmouth and Salterton
1. 7.1903	Ashton to Exeter
6. 7.1903	Chacewater to Blackwater
24. 8.1903	Axminster and Lyme Regis
2. 1.1905	Perranporth to Newquay
1. 5.1908	Bideford, Westward Ho! and Appledore